W9-CSQ-241

Linda Granfield

REMEMBERING JOHN MCCRAE

SOLDIER·DOCTOR·POET

Scholastic Canada Ltd.
Toronto New York London Auckland Sydney
Mexico City New Delhi Hong Kong Buenos Aires

For Ron Waldie,
Friend, supporter, and forever our "best man"

Scholastic Canada Ltd.
604 King Street West, Toronto, Ontario M5V 1E1, Canada

Scholastic Inc.
557 Broadway, New York, NY 10012, USA

Scholastic Australia Pty Limited
PO Box 579, Gosford, NSW 2250, Australia

Scholastic New Zealand Limited
Private Bag 94407, Greenmount, Auckland, New Zealand

Scholastic Children's Books
Euston House, 24 Eversholt Street, London NW1 1DB, UK

Library and Archives Canada Cataloguing in Publication

Granfield, Linda
Remembering John McCrae : soldier, doctor, poet /
Linda Granfield.

ISBN 978-0-439-93561-6 (bound).— ISBN 978-0-439-93560-9 (pbk.)

1. McCrae, John, 1872-1918--Juvenile literature.
2. Physicians--Canada--Biography--Juvenile literature.
3. Soldiers--Canada--Biography--Juvenile literature.
4. Poets, Canadian (English)--Biography--Juvenile literature.
I. Title.
FC556.M42G72 2009   j971.061'2092   C2009-901171-9

ISBN-10 0-439-93561-X (bound).— ISBN-10 0-439-93560-1 (pbk.)

6 5 4 3 2 1   Printed in Singapore   09 10 11 12 13

JOHN McCRAE's "In Flanders Fields" is called the most popular poem of the First World War (1914–1918). Millions of people around the world recite or sing the lines every year during remembrance ceremonies. Many of us know "the poppy poem." But who was John McCrae?

A copy of "In Flanders Fields" hand-written by John McCrae.

Badge—CLUB MOSS

Arms

THE CLAN TARTAN

FORTITER

CLAN MACRAE

The McCraes, like other Scottish families, or clans, have a specific tartan design that identifies them.

Eilean Donan ("Island of Donan") Castle near Dornie, Scotland, is the ancestral home of the McCraes. The castle, first established in the thirteenth century, was destroyed in 1719 and was restored over 200 years later.

Baby Jack McCrae. In this formal portrait, he clutches a soft toy and wears an embroidered dress. (At this time, boys wore dresses until they were about two years old.) Jack's silver baby cup is decorated with ivy, which represents growth and eternal life. This was an important symbol, since many babies born in the 1800s did not survive due to illness.

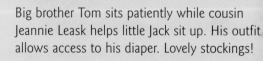

Big brother Tom sits patiently while cousin Jeannie Leask helps little Jack sit up. His outfit allows access to his diaper. Lovely stockings!

JOHN McCRAE was born on November 30, 1872, in a small stone house near the banks of the Speed River in Guelph, Ontario. His grandfather, Thomas McCrae, emigrated to Canada from Scotland in 1849. Thomas operated a local sawmill. Ten years later he owned the Guelph Woollen Mills. John's father David worked at the woollen mills, but later became a farmer and prize-winning cattle breeder. In 1870 he married Janet Eckford, a minister's daughter. The family grew to include three children: brothers Thomas and John — called Jack — and sister Geills *(jheels)*.

Click! Jack's about three years old and wears a jacket, short pants . . . and a very serious expression.

Janet McCrae shared her love of books with her children. They sang "Frog Went A-Courtin'" (or "Frog Went A-Wooing"), a traditional English folk song. In 1880 Jack wrote to his cousin John Gow: *Tomorrow is my 8th birthday. Geills . . . can sing about Miss Mousie sat on [F]roggie's knee.*

Family photos of long ago were formal, unlike the more casual ones we usually see today. Sitting still for long periods to pose for photographs could make the subject look a little stiff.

JOHN ENJOYED some of the activities other boys liked during the late 1800s — reading adventure stories in the popular *The Boy's Own Paper*, making sketches, creating scrapbook pages, writing to pen pals. He spent time caring for and watching the antics of some of the animals at "Janefield," the family farm at the edge of Guelph. Stam, Lady Christabel and Puss Nell were just a few of the McCraes' cows, dogs, horses and cats. Most were work animals, some were pets.

John enjoyed nature. He spent part of his boyhood summers fishing, catching butterflies, and hunting for milk snakes.

Janet McCrae with Tom (right), Geills and John, around 1881. The boys are young enough to wear knickerbockers ("knickers" or short pants), stockings and boots. The shift from wearing knickers to long trousers was a big milestone in a boy's life.

The adventure stories John read in *The Boy's Own Paper* encouraged him and other boys to crave excitement. The popular magazine also featured history, science, craft projects and plenty of poetry.

Janefield, the home of John McCrae's grandparents, was later inherited by his father, David.

Skating on Guelph's Speed River (above) was a popular winter pastime for John and his friends. This postcard (left) from around 1900 shows a boy wearing knickerbockers.
  Some skates from the era (below) were not like modern ones, but blades tied on over boots.

"*I was at Westminster Abbey today.*"

THE McCRAE CHILDREN grew up in a devout Presbyterian home. Their parents respected learning and held the belief that each person had a duty to God and country. By the age of twelve, John was enrolled at Guelph Collegiate Institute for his high school education. He was also becoming involved in the military life that his father was devoted to.

John practised drills and marching with the Highland Cadet Corps at the collegiate. His dedication to his military life earned him a gold medal honouring him as the best-drilled cadet in Ontario in 1887.

John's interest in school and cadet duties, as well as in the St. Andrew's Church community, still left him time to enjoy sports and to travel abroad with his father. After visiting Westminster Abbey in London, England, in May of 1886 he wrote to his sister, Geills: *I was at Westminster Abbey [today]. It is where the Kings and Queens are buried and big people. I do not mean people over six feet . . .*

Thomas (top) and John (left) often spent time with relatives who lived elsewhere in Ontario, like their cousin Walter Gow. All ages took part in letter-writing and exchanging formal photographs with friends and family.

Photographs taken throughout his life show John in a variety of military uniforms.

6

John kept scrapbooks filled with interesting bits and pieces of his daily life. On this page (far left) from one of his scrapbooks we see his youthful interest in ships, lovely ladies and dramatic scenes. The careful arrangement shows his developing artistic talent.

John holds a watermelon waiting to be carved. A little bit of practise for a future surgeon?

Young people socialized and learned about nature on trips such as this "botanical outing." They hiked through the woods, identified plants and rocks, and took specimens home. These members of the Guelph Scientific Society are on a walk at Rockwood, Ontario. John is on the far right, second row. His parents (top row, right side) acted as chaperones. Casual clothing would have been unthinkable in the 1890s. Even in the woods!

THE GLOBE TRAIN PASSING DUNDAS.

CANADIAN PACIFIC RAILWAY

Railways reached right across Canada, and like many boys his age, John looked forward to journeys by ship and train. Exciting stories about the adventures to be found "on the rails" often appeared in magazines.

Time for university studies to begin

University graduation, 1894 — time for medical school studies to begin. Tutoring other students helped pay John's education expenses.

John attended University College at the University of Toronto.

(Right) Ready for an outing, university student John McCrae sports a stylish Homburg, a hat made popular by Edward VII before he became king in 1901. (Left) Tom and John, this time wearing bowler hats, stroll through Toronto's High Park.

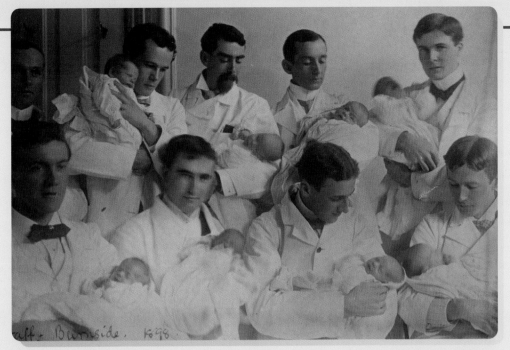

Young Dr. McCrae (bottom row, far right) cradles a newborn at Burnside Lying-In Hospital, Toronto, in 1898.

JOHN, AT AGE SIXTEEN, enrolled at the University of Toronto, where his older brother, Tom, was already studying. He left the quiet of Janefield and soon enjoyed the bustle of a big city with lots to keep two brothers busy in and out of the classroom. They rented rooms close to the university and ate their meals at a nearby restaurant. They joined the Varsity Glee Club and the Zeta Psi Fraternity. John and Tom also played on the varsity rugby team — and suffered their share of injuries on the playing field. John was peeved by newspaper accounts that frequently misspelled his last name, but he enjoyed being mentioned: *It is said by the* Mail *that "the two McCraes" distinguished themselves etc. Whoop!*

John suffered throughout his life from asthma. Toronto's soot-filled air caused his health to fail, so he took a year off from his studies (1892–93). Instead, he worked as a resident master in Mathematics at the Ontario Agricultural College in Guelph. But John turned out to be too young for the job and couldn't cope. He returned to Toronto.

After completing his undergraduate studies at the University of Toronto, John stayed on to study medicine.

There, some of the best doctors and medical teachers in the world practised.

John gained valuable experience by working with a Guelph doctor and family friend during his summer vacations. His medical studies at the University of Toronto were completed in 1898. He was the top student in his class when he graduated.

WITH GREAT EXCITEMENT, John McCrae left Toronto to work at Johns Hopkins Hospital in Baltimore, Maryland. There, some of the best doctors and medical teachers in the world practised. His brother Tom was also a doctor on staff, but was studying in Germany when John arrived in 1899.

Sir William Osler, a Canadian regarded as one of the greatest doctors in the history of modern medicine, was a professor at Johns Hopkins when John McCrae arrived there. Osler was a "hands-on" teacher who thought it was better for doctors to spend time in laboratory work, and listening to and observing their patients, rather than sitting in lecture halls.

John enjoyed the Oslers' hospitality. He also exchanged letters and shared friendships with people such as Laura Kains, but there were no lasting romantic relationships. It is believed that John had been in love during his university years, but that the young woman died. Despite the best matchmaking efforts of his friends and family, and his busy social life, John never married.

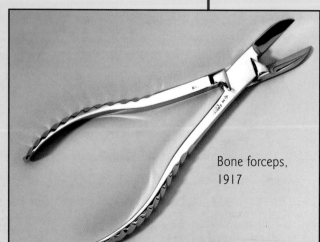

Bone forceps, 1917

Dr. Osler's only child, Edward Revere Osler (here shown riding piggy-back on his father), was killed in the First World War. John had known Revere since the boy was young.

John once wrote a teasing note to Laura Kains: *I never knew you had as many sisters as you say you have in the last letter. Are they all as good-looking as — excuse me, you will be vain, so I shall change the subject.*

Johns Hopkins Hospital in 1899

John McCrae in 1901, after his return from South Africa.

Our Boys Return.

Lieut. John McCrae,
Gun. " F. Abbs,
" S. Barber,
" T. Bargett,
" D. Hilton,
" C. Fennell,
" W. Cartlidge,
" J. Cormack,
" H. Denyes,
" W. Gavin,
" J. Gleister,
" J. Gokey,
" H. Howe,
" K. Lett,
" J. Macdonald,
" A. Miller,
" D. McGibbon,
" B. McKenzie,
" W. Partridge,
" J. Philp,
" J. Sparrow,
" B. Stephenson,
" E. Sutton,
" H. Thomas,
" J. Wallace,
" M. Wideman,

WELCOME HOME
January, 1901.

After landing in Cape Town and living in a tent city in the shadow of Table Mountain, John McCrae and D Battery of the Royal Canadian Artillery marched to the Transvaal and Orange Free State areas. In 1902, when the war ended, the two republics became British colonies that later formed part of the Union of South Africa.

WHEN THE BOER WAR began, John had already been involved in militia units in Guelph and Toronto. A keen supporter of the British Empire, he put off planned post-graduate studies in Montreal and volunteered for service as a member of the Royal Canadian Artillery.

The Boers were white South Africans of Dutch descent who lived in two small South African republics, Transvaal and the Orange Free State. When gold was discovered in South Africa, British prospectors rushed there to make their fortunes — something the Boers resented. They declared war against Britain later that year and the South African War, also known as the Second Boer War, began.

Soon after arriving in Cape Town, South Africa, Lieutenant John McCrae wrote to his family: *I am getting quite used to soldiering now; feel as if I were born to it.*

Still, John had a tough year. He nearly drowned while fording a stream on horseback when he fell into the water and his horse toppled on him. He and the other troops spent hours each day crossing South Africa's vast territories in heat and wind. They went without food and fought the

as if I were born to it."

enemy in battles and ambushes. He missed home — and regular meals, as seen in this letter to his family in March 1900: *[W]ouldn't I just like to sit down to tea [with] you all. I think of Geills's whipped cream & strawberry jam and lots of bread & butter. Hooray! Some day it will come.*

The British forces were victorious in some battles but defeated in others. In January 1901, John McCrae, called "a brilliant young officer," returned to Canada and was promoted to captain, and a year later, to major. He gave public lectures about "Artillery and its Employment in South Africa."

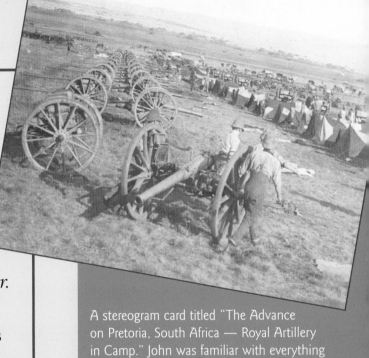

A stereogram card titled "The Advance on Pretoria, South Africa — Royal Artillery in Camp." John was familiar with everything seen in this picture: tents, field guns, cork helmets — and Pretoria.

Artists depicted battles for newspaper readers back home. The action on these sandy, parched battlefields of South Africa recalls illustrations in *The Boy's Own Paper*. On one march, John travelled 769 kilometres through the hot, dry Great Karoo Desert.

"*I feel as if I didn't want to see a sick person*

WHEN HE RETURNED to Canada after the South African War, John worked in Montreal for four years on the advanced medical studies he had postponed. Meanwhile, he also served as a visiting professor of Pathology (the study of the nature of disease) at the University of Vermont until 1911.

In Montreal he was appointed an associate of medicine at the Royal Victoria Hospital, and was also a lecturer at McGill University, educating future doctors. Students found him a patient teacher who had a talent for making difficult subjects easier to understand and who seldom lost his temper in class.

Despite his busy schedule, John also worked as a pathologist at Montreal General Hospital, as a doctor for the Royal Alexandra Hospital for Infectious Diseases, and in his own private practice. During his time in Montreal he performed hundreds of autopsies and co-wrote an 878-page textbook about pathology. He donated his pathology specimens and his records to the medical museum on the McGill campus, where they can still be viewed. He wrote to his friend, Dr. Oskar Klotz: . . . *usual spring tiredness — I feel as if I didn't want to see a sick person or a student at all.*

Busy as he was as a doctor and teacher, John remained a member of a local Presbyterian church,

The mansions of the business barons Montreal lined both sides of Sherbrook Street (above). John lived in the home of his friend and colleague Dr. Edward Archibald on nearby Metcalfe Street, just a few blocks from the university and the hospitals.

John McCrae did not like spending unnecessarily on his wardrobe. *Jack McCrae . . . is so nice, but . . . why does he always insist on wearing clothes six sizes too small for him?* wrote one acquaintance. At the hospitals, a long white laboratory coat covered his ill-fitting clothes.

or a student at all."

as well as several Montreal social groups, including the Shakespeare Club and the Pen and Pencil Club. There he met Canadian writer and humorist Stephen Leacock.

During the hot city summers he relaxed at the Murray Bay (La Malbaie) area in Quebec with the Osler family. He travelled to Europe. He fished. His humour and storytelling got him invitations to dinners in the homes of Montreal's most influential families. All John's efforts were pointing towards success.

The brass office sign for Dr. John McCrae's private practice.

Dr. McCrae (far right) instructs a class at the Royal Alexandra Hospital. His cap and the students' hooded gowns were worn to limit the amount of bacteria that might be spread. In the early twentieth century, infectious diseases like measles and scarlet fever killed many people. Today, thanks to the work done by pathologists such as John McCrae, vaccines prevent such deaths.

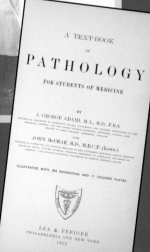

A TEXT-BOOK
OF
PATHOLOGY
FOR STUDENTS OF MEDICINE

BY

J. GEORGE ADAMI, M.A., M.D., F.R.S.

AND

JOHN McCRAE, M.D., M.R.C.P. (LOND.)

ILLUSTRATED WITH 304 ENGRAVINGS AND 11 COLORED PLATES

LEA & FEBIGER
PHILADELPHIA AND NEW YORK
1912

The expedition travelled thousands of kilometres over lakes, rivers, muskeg and rock. The trip ended in Quebec City in mid-September 1910. From there, John returned to Montreal.

IN EARLY AUGUST 1910, John had the opportunity to explore Hudson Bay. Earl Grey, Canada's governor general, had invited him to be the on-duty doctor for an expedition heading north to York Factory and beyond. The government wished to establish a new port to help bring Canadian wheat to England via Hudson Bay.

Thirty-eight men began the long journey at Norway House in Manitoba. Along the route, Cree guides paddled twelve 7-metre canoes down rapids and carried them over a number of portages. Grey's group was greeted warmly and offered help by aboriginal peoples along the way. Unfortunately, Grey found that the proposed site for the port was not suitable after all, but the expedition carried on with the remainder of their journey.

Most of the trip was enjoyable. But at one point John wrote in his diary: *We landed on a marshy flat . . . wet with marsh bottom & mosquitoes beyond speaking . . . A bare hand gets a dozen in a minute.*

John McCrae carried a pocket-sized diary with him on the expedition. Beside his sketch of an Inuit woman is this caption: *The average boy and women dressed alike. Tho' the women add a . . . skirt down to the knees.* He noted that a walrus was killed "and eaten on the spot by the whole crowd." On another page he remarks that papooses [babies] are wrapped "with dried moss by way of diaper."

the [1001 stories] of the Arabian nights."

The group sailed in the governor general's steamship for the last part of the journey. As they skirted the coasts of the Atlantic provinces, they spotted icebergs and reindeer, as well as Nova Scotia's imposing Fortress of Louisbourg. In Prince Edward Island they invited Lucy Maud Montgomery, the author of *Anne of Green Gables,* to dinner. Her book had been published two years before, and Earl Grey was a fan who wanted to meet her.

By mid-September, the journey was completed. Earl Grey wrote to thank John McCrae, but not just for his medical skills en route: *You were able to beat the record of the [1001 stories] of the Arabian nights, for I believe the 3000 miles of our travels were illumined by as many stories [told by you].*

Members of the expedition took photographs to document their journey. Earl Grey, hands clasped, leans against a post on the porch at the Norway House residence. John McCrae, the only hatless figure in the group, sits waiting to resume smoking his pipe.

The Hudson Bay Company's Norway House, on Lake Winnipeg, Manitoba, is named for the Norwegians who built the supply post in the early 1800s. At right is a sketch John drew of the Archway warehouse with its bell.

Norway House

Words were important to him.

Feet up, with a book. A bit of rest for Dr. McCrae, wearing his medical whites, while off duty at the Robert Garrett Hospital for Children in Mount Airy, Maryland, 189

JANET McCRAE ONCE WROTE to a friend about John: *I always rated Jack — first, the soldier, second, the student, and third the physician — and 4th, 5th, or 6th, the poet.*

John would have agreed with the ranking of soldier in first place. His list would have put doctor next, closely followed by writer. Words were important to him, whether they appeared in a medical journal or a book of verse. He read constantly throughout his life, during breaks from hospital rounds in Canada or wherever he was posted abroad.

He enjoyed the latest popular novels by authors like Robert Louis Stevenson *(Treasure Island)*. New books were always welcome gifts. And while John never wrote a novel, he *did* write stories and poetry that were published from the time he was in university.

In his early twenties, he entered a writing competition sponsored by a newspaper and won the grand sum of $25 (almost $600 today). Like many writers, then and now, he complained about how little payment he received for his work. He also disliked the illustrations placed with his stories (unless, of course, he had drawn them!).

Readers always enjoy meeting a favourite writer. Rudyard Kipling, author of *The Jungle Book* and many other stories, was one of the most popular writers in the world during John's lifetime. While in South Africa, John and two friends heard that Kipling was at an elegant Cape Town hotel and went there to see him. They missed him, but then their luck changed and Kipling chatted with them.

The Harvest of the Sea
By John M'Crae

John illustrated one of his early published poems and signed it with his "artist's mark" — a *J* interlocked with an *M* (inset).

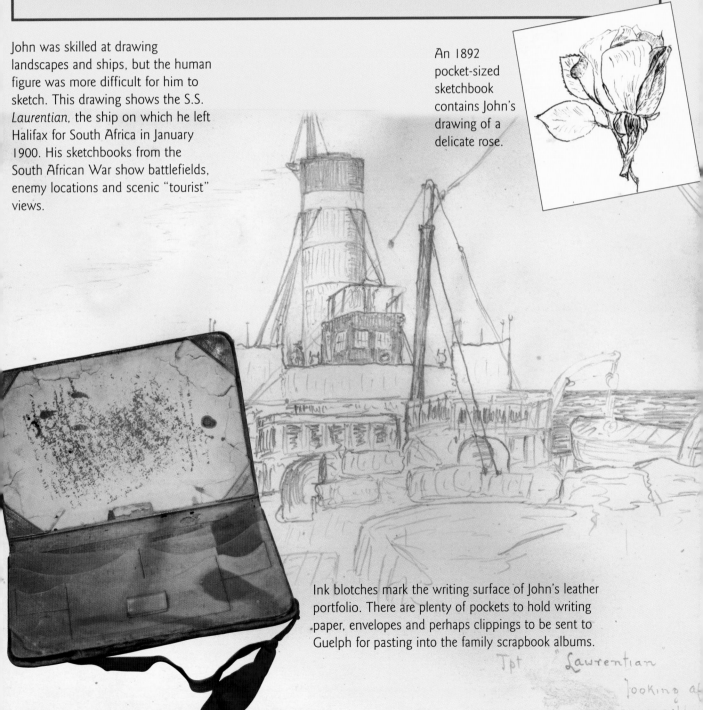

John never lacked a healthy ego — he believed in the quality of each piece he mailed to magazines in Canada and Great Britain. His poetry and art reflected his sensitivity to everything around him — the deaths of friends, nature, the sea. But something of much greater importance was looming on the horizon, something that would inspire John . . . and that would involve the whole world.

John was skilled at drawing landscapes and ships, but the human figure was more difficult for him to sketch. This drawing shows the S.S. *Laurentian,* the ship on which he left Halifax for South Africa in January 1900. His sketchbooks from the South African War show battlefields, enemy locations and scenic "tourist" views.

An 1892 pocket-sized sketchbook contains John's drawing of a delicate rose.

Ink blotches mark the writing surface of John's leather portfolio. There are plenty of pockets to hold writing paper, envelopes and perhaps clippings to be sent to Guelph for pasting into the family scrapbook albums.

Tpt "Laurentian Jooking a
26/1/00

Mending thousands of wounded

This portrait is the best-known image of John McCrae. It was taken at the William Notman & Son studio in Montreal before John left Canada for the Great War.

WHEN BRITAIN declared war against Germany on August 4, 1914, John McCrae was on a ship bound for England and some holiday time. After the war news arrived, however, the ship ran without its lights so that German submarines could not find it. Once he arrived in England, John quickly contacted officials and offered his services as either a soldier or as a doctor.

His age (forty-one) worked against him as a soldier, as did the fact that he had resigned from military life in 1904. But he was appointed surgeon in the 1st Brigade Artillery and soon returned to Montreal to prepare for duty. Scheduled to leave Canada, he wrote to his sister to say that he would not go home to Guelph to see his parents. He believed that his mother would become too upset, "and we can hope for happier times."

John McCrae, newly promoted to lieutenant colonel, treated soldiers' wounds at the Second Battle of Ypres in Belgium (April 22 – May 25, 1915). There he served primarily as a surgeon, but also assisted the artillery operations. That summer he was moved to the No. 3 Canadian General Hospital near Boulogne-sur-Mer, France.

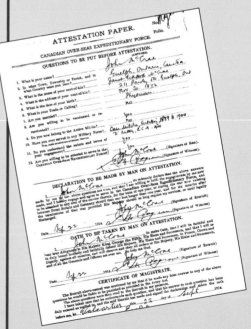

When a soldier enlisted he filled in a form called an Attestation Paper that confirmed under oath that the facts given on the form were true. John McCrae's paper shows that he was 6 feet (about 2 metres) tall, had blue eyes and brown hair, and had an appendicitis scar.

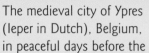

The medieval city of Ypres (Ieper in Dutch), Belgium, in peaceful days before the war. Pictures of Ypres taken after the war reveal total destruction. The thirteenth-century Cloth Hall (above) was restored and now houses a major First World War museum.

McGill University doctors and nurses staffed this "tent town," as the newspapers called it. In October 1915, the hospital had 900 beds, 4 ambulances (gifts from "the ladies of Canada"), an X-ray department and an operating theatre where John worked.

Winds off the nearby English Channel tore at the flimsy canvas. In early 1916, the hospital moved into an abandoned, ruined Jesuit college in Boulogne. There John worked for the rest of his war, mending the thousands of wounded he could, and sending others back to England for further recuperation and possible return to action. (England was called "Old Blighty" by the troops. A wound that got them sent there, away from battle, was often called "a Blighty.") Although dedicated to his medical duties, John would rather have been with the artillery at the Front, only 60 kilometres away.

Dr. McCrae strikes a jaunty pose beside a sundial. This photo, believed to be the last of John McCrae as a civilian, was taken in the summer of 1914 in the garden of a friend in Cambridge, Massachusetts.

Here at the Essex Farm dressing station, John McCrae tended the wounded brought from the battlefield at Ypres. The doorway and lanterns provided the only light. The floor, made of earth from manure-filled farm fields, spread bacteria that infected soldiers' wounds.

"We really expected to die in our tracks."

Always a frequent letter writer, John told family and friends about the battles at Ypres in the spring of 1915: *We stayed 17 days and nights, and it was HELL all the time.... We really expected to die in our tracks. We never had our boots off, much less our clothes.*

The wounded needed to be treated whenever they arrived, as John wrote to a friend on New Year's Eve day, 1916: *Xmas Day we had 1300 patients in.... I have a hundred beds on my own hands as well as supervision: we have had a good deal of illness.*

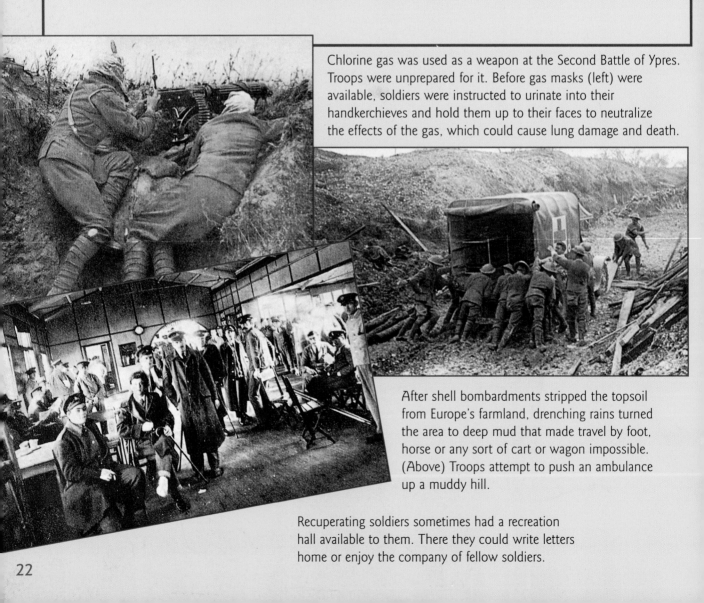

Chlorine gas was used as a weapon at the Second Battle of Ypres. Troops were unprepared for it. Before gas masks (left) were available, soldiers were instructed to urinate into their handkerchieves and hold them up to their faces to neutralize the effects of the gas, which could cause lung damage and death.

After shell bombardments stripped the topsoil from Europe's farmland, drenching rains turned the area to deep mud that made travel by foot, horse or any sort of cart or wagon impossible. (Above) Troops attempt to push an ambulance up a muddy hill.

Recuperating soldiers sometimes had a recreation hall available to them. There they could write letters home or enjoy the company of fellow soldiers.

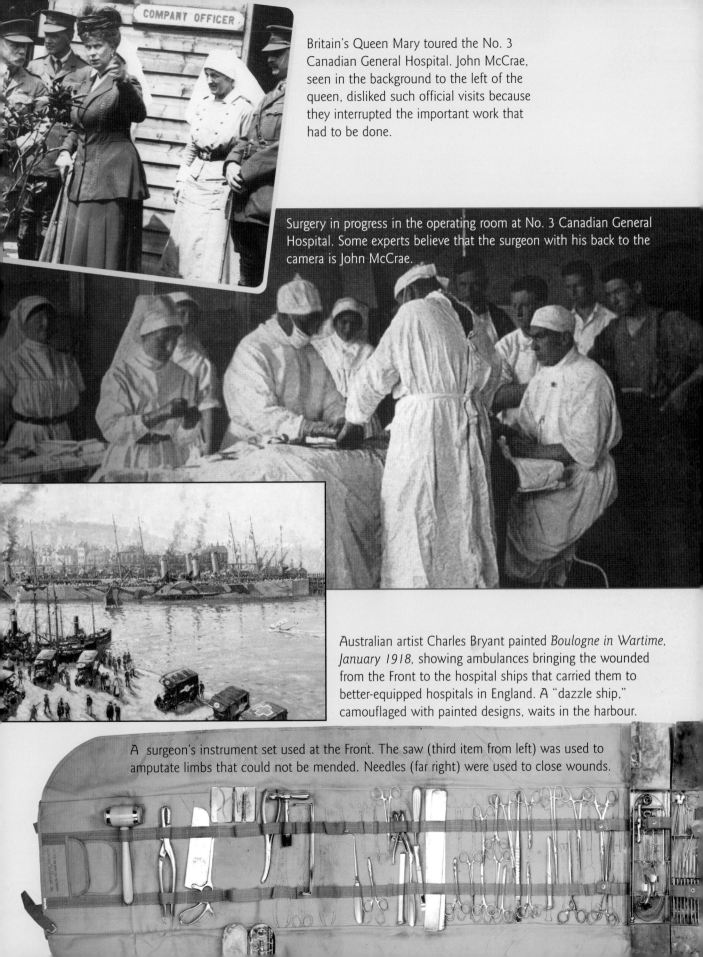

Britain's Queen Mary toured the No. 3 Canadian General Hospital. John McCrae, seen in the background to the left of the queen, disliked such official visits because they interrupted the important work that had to be done.

Surgery in progress in the operating room at No. 3 Canadian General Hospital. Some experts believe that the surgeon with his back to the camera is John McCrae.

Australian artist Charles Bryant painted *Boulogne in Wartime, January 1918*, showing ambulances bringing the wounded from the Front to the hospital ships that carried them to better-equipped hospitals in England. A "dazzle ship," camouflaged with painted designs, waits in the harbour.

A surgeon's instrument set used at the Front. The saw (third item from left) was used to amputate limbs that could not be mended. Needles (far right) were used to close wounds.

CHILDREN AND ANIMALS

delighted John McCrae. When he visited London as a teenager, John wrote home asking after the Janefield pets. While at war in South Africa, he wrote to Geills to again ask about favourite animals back in Guelph.

His reports about the young children he cared for at Mount Airy hospital are touching. His nieces and nephews enjoyed humorous notes and sketches from "Uncle Jack," and the children of the Archibald family he lived with in Montreal giggled at the silly names he called them. "Peglegs alias Slip McGloover" was one of them.

Sir Andrew Macphail, John McCrae's friend and first biographer, wrote: *Through all his life . . . dogs and children followed [McCrae] as shadows follow men. To walk in the streets with him was a slow procession. Every dog and every child one met must be spoken to.*

In one of his last letters to Canada, John mentioned Windy, *a nice big old dog [that] came off the hospital train with his labels tied on his collar and his second wound — a broken leg.* John wrote that when Windy died: *[he was given] a decent burial and headboard in our woods. How one hates to lose the faithful beasts!*

A magnificent horse was prized by any soldier. John's horse, Bonfire, was a gift from a friend. Bonfire was wounded twice and carried his master throughout the war. In December 1915, John wrote to Geills: *I wish you could meet [Bonfire]: he is one of the dearest things in horses that one could find. . . . he puts up his lips to your face & gives a kind of foolish waffle of his lower lip that is very comical.*

one could find."

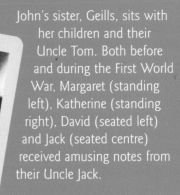

John's sister, Geills, sits with her children and their Uncle Tom. Both before and during the First World War, Margaret (standing left), Katherine (standing right), David (seated left) and Jack (seated centre) received amusing notes from their Uncle Jack.

For ΚATHERINE ΚILGOUЯ

The place for jam

Is on the plate.

And here it gives me pain to state

That I have known

A certain place

Where children have it

On the face.

That is what goops

Are apt to do.

I hope it's not

At all like you!

DON'T BE A ƆOOꟼ!!!

"Bonfire" his mark

Despite the heavy workload Dr. McCrae had at the military hospital, he wrote many letters to his sister's children. The letters were supposedly written by Bonfire (or Bonneau) and were signed by a horseshoe (or a paw print) instead of Uncle Jack's name.

During wartime, soldiers often welcomed the warmth and friendship of local family pets. Bonneau was a setter that belonged to the *concièrge* at the hospital where John worked. He wrote that the dog: *now belong[s] to Bonfire. . . . They are very pretty together and are very fond of one another.* John had this postcard photo made and sent it to a friend in Canada.

CARTE POSTALE

Correspondance   Adresse

"Bonneau"   his mark

He was deeply touched by the death of a friend.

The officers of the 1st Brigade, Canadian Field Artillery, posed outside of their mess at the Bear Inn in Devizes, England. John McCrae is in the front row, left, and Alexis Helmer is in the back row, fifth from the left, holding the iron pillar.

(Left to right) Capt. Lawrence Cosgrave, Lt. Col. Edward Morrison, and Lt. Col. John McCrae. Cosgrave watched his friend write "In Flanders Fields."

IN THE EARLY MORNING of May 2, 1915, twenty-two-year-old Lt. Alexis Helmer was checking a Canadian position along the Yser Canal during the long Second Battle of Ypres. The medieval Belgian city was in blackened ruins. A German shell exploded at Helmer's feet, killing him instantly. His remains were buried in nearby Essex Farm Cemetery, as his friend John McCrae recited prayers. John and the others went back to their duties and Helmer's grave was marked with a wooden cross.

Helmer's death inspired John McCrae to write "In Flanders Fields" the following day. Lawrence Miller Cosgrave, present when John wrote the poem, said that Helmer's grave "was a sad but magnificent sight. . . . [McCrae] composed the poem in twenty minutes."

There are different accounts of exactly how and where John wrote the poem. Whether he sat on an ambulance step, or outside a dugout, matters little. What does matter is that he was deeply touched by the death of a friend and was in a setting of hastily built cemeteries, spring poppies (a flower symbolic of sleep), and birds singing despite the deafening roar of battle. In this poem, the last verse calls upon the living to join the war effort so that Helmer and millions like him would not have perished in vain. Victory could be, would be, achieved.

The poem's popularity after its publication later in 1915 was huge. Agencies and individuals asked to reproduce it. At the end of 1916, John wrote to his mother: *Yesterday a [telegram] asking permission to sell ["Flanders Fields"] at a bazaar in Boston. So it goes.*

In 1917, another of his poems, "The Anxious Dead," was published. Some believe this poem to be better than "In Flanders Fields," but John wrote to his mother: *[I]t will hardly go as far as "Flanders Fields," I think.* He was correct. "In Flanders Fields" has overshadowed all his other poetry.

Alexis Helmer's grave disappeared as the war continued. The constant bombardment of the earth, and harsh weather, washed quickly painted names from temporary markers, causing many graves to become those "known only to God."

Helmer's name is carved into the walls of the Menin Gate Memorial in Ypres, along with those of nearly 55,000 other men who were lost without a trace. Each night at eight o'clock, Alexis Helmer and the others are remembered as buglers play "The Last Post" on silver trumpets during a simple ceremony at the Gate.

Alexis Helmer (1892–1915) grew up in Ottawa. He attended McGill University and received a degree in civil engineering before the war began.

IN FLANDERS FIELDS.

In Flanders fields the poppies blow
Between the crosses, row on row,
   That mark our place; and in the sky
   The larks, still bravely singing, fly
Scarce heard amid the guns below.

We are the Dead.   Short days ago
We lived, felt dawn, saw sunset glow,
   Loved and were loved, and now we lie
      In Flanders fields.

Take up our quarrel with the foe:
To you from failing hands we throw
   The torch; be yours to hold it high.
   If ye break faith with us who die
We shall not sleep, though poppies grow
      In Flanders fields.

The public first saw "In Flanders Fields" in the December 8, 1915, edition of *Punch*, a British humour magazine that was published from 1841 until 2002. John McCrae's name did not appear with the poem.

In 1917, lines from "In Flanders Fields" were used on posters and other advertisements for Canadian war fundraising. Here, an ink blotter urges the owner to "Buy Victory Bonds." These bonds raised over $400 million.

John McCrae during what may have been his last photographic session. On this December day in 1917, John chuckles as Bonneau (right foreground) swishes his tail. Bonfire cooperates for the photographer.

After John McCrae's death, Bonfire was sold and the proceeds were given to Janet McCrae. She later donated the money to a campaign to place a memorial seat at the Wimereux Communal Cemetery in France.

"He knew it was 'the end.'"

BY THE SUMMER OF 1917, John McCrae was suffering from the years of dealing with the wounded and dying. His asthma was relentless, his cheerfulness replaced with weariness. On January 23, 1918, he became ill. The next day he was told he had been appointed consulting doctor to the First British Army, an enormous honour. On January 25, he was moved from his Boulogne hospital to the officers' hospital in Wimereux, a small town just 5 kilometres north. John himself had diagnosed pneumonia. Meningitis was also suspected. The clouds of gas at Ypres years before had no doubt weakened his asthmatic lungs. John was worried, and a nurse later reported, "He said he knew it was 'the end.'"

Only three days after becoming so ill, John McCrae lost consciousness. He died in the early morning hours of January 28, 1918. Nurses who had worked with him in both the Montreal and the military hospitals lamented that they wished they "could have done something to show our appreciation. . . . He has gone never knowing how much we cared."

The next day, on a sunny afternoon, Lt. Col. John McCrae was buried with full military honours. Officers and friends walked the kilometre and a half to the

John McCrae once wrote: *I have a very deep affection for Bonfire, for we have been through so much together.* Bonfire followed McCrae's flag-draped casket in the funeral procession. His master's boots are reversed in the stirrups, a symbol of respect showing that the fallen soldier will not ride again — instead, he is looking back for one last time. White-capped nursing sisters stand solemnly on the left as the officers salute.

Sturdy marble stones have replaced the weather-beaten wooden grave markers.

cemetery. After prayers and a bugler's rendition of "The Last Post," John was laid to rest beneath heaps of floral wreaths. His father later wrote to a cousin: *You may not know that we have lost [our son] John — Jack we called him.*

Four years after John McCrae left Canada to join the war, and nearly ten months after his death, the fighting stopped. At the eleventh hour of the eleventh day of the eleventh month, the Armistice was signed to end the Great War. Families would soon be welcoming home their soldiers. The business of rebuilding the world would begin. In Guelph, Ontario, Canada, the McCrae family began to heal. John McCrae, soldier, doctor and poet, remained in Flanders' fields.

The cemetery in Wimereux, France, overlooked the English Channel. It was the final resting place of British Commonwealth soldiers like John McCrae and members of the local community. The first marker placed on John's grave was like the others, a wooden cross with a metal nameplate.

Daniel Chester French designed this bronze sculpture called "In Flanders Fields" as a tribute to the men of Milton, Massachusetts, who died during the First World War. The monument was unveiled in 1925.

NEARLY ONE HUNDRED YEARS after it was written, "In Flanders Fields" remains as popular as when it was first published. David McCrae wrote in 1918: *[Jack] had written a bit — "In Flanders Fields" . . . which has since been much copied and quoted — it is one of the poems of the war.*

During the Great War, professional and amateur poets "answered" the poem's final lines, pledging that the torch would be passed. The loss of so many soldiers would not be forgotten.

Sculptors, composers and artists have interpreted the poem for new generations. Its poignant lines were used on Second World War (1939–1945) posters and have since appeared in films and on various websites. The poem has been recorded by actors and musicians around the world.

John McCrae, the Canadian soldier and doctor who wrote those fifteen remarkable lines, created a poem that continues to inspire us and call us to action.

In 2001 the Bank of Canada issued a ten-dollar note featuring the first verse of "In Flanders Fields" in English and French.

Peace gardens and memorials around the world feature the poem or portions of it on bronze or stone tablets. The symbol of the torch is often incorporated. This memorial garden, featuring a bronze book inscribed with the poem, and a huge torch, is next to John McCrae's birthplace in Guelph, Ontario.

A poem that continues to inspire us

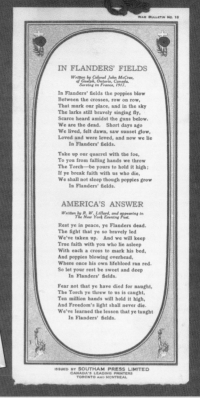

"America's Answer" by R. W. Lillard was just one of the international replies to John McCrae's poem. The McCrae family collected various decorated printings of the poem in their scrapbooks. A musical version of the poem was written by John Philip Sousa while John McCrae was still alive.

A stained-glass window (left) in the Strathcona Anatomy and Dentistry Building (above) at McGill University commemorates John McCrae as a faculty member who died in the First World War.

When someone pins a poppy on a lapel...

Two early versions of the Earl Haig poppy. A 1930 newspaper article noted that in eleven months, veterans in England had made 40 million poppies for November 11.

Visitors place wreaths of poppies and small wooden crosses on John McCrae's grave each year, particularly around Remembrance Day.

Douglas Haig, 1st Earl Haig, commanded the British Expeditionary Force for most of the First World War. Later, he helped found the Royal British Legion and supported the distribution of poppies to provide assistance for ex-servicemen.

THE SCARLET CORN POPPY has become a symbol of life throughout the world. During the First World War the bright flowers, heavy-headed and blowing in the early summer breezes, continued to bloom despite the destruction of the European countryside. Through the churned-up, muddy battlefields rose a sea of red blossoms, the colour of life's blood, moving where all had been stilled by war and death.

When John McCrae died, a fellow doctor reported that the nurses at the military hospital looked for poppies to put on his grave. And the world did not wait until after John's death to begin wearing the red flowers. In 1916, posters were already urging the public to remember and to aid the wounded and disabled servicemen returning from the world's battlefields: *Poppy Day — Wear a Flanders Poppy.*

British and American Legions adopted the poppy as their memorial flower. During the 1920s, artificial poppies raised money from millions of people around the world. The donations were used to help rehabilitate the returning veterans of the Great War.

In Canada, John McCrae's homeland, there was talk of replacing the country's

Volunteers in this 1920s photograph carry trays of red poppies and cans for donations. A British Legion car nearby is decorated with poppy garlands.

symbol, the maple leaf, with the scarlet poppy. An English newspaper stated in a November 1921 edition: *[N]ature has sown it thickly over the graves of our dead, and with it one of the noblest poems of the war is connected.*

While John McCrae urged his readers to take up the torch of battle and enter the fray, another more symbolic torch, one of remembrance, continues to shine brightly around the world whenever someone pins a red poppy on a lapel and reflects upon the cost of freedom.

A glass magic-lantern slide, of the same poster, would have been used at public meetings to encourage donations for poppies.

Significant Events in the Life of

NOVEMBER 30, 1872 John (Jack) McCrae is born in Guelph, Ontario, Canada

1878–1888 attends Guelph Central School and Guelph Collegiate Institute

1888 begins undergraduate studies at the University of Toronto

1894 graduates from the University of Toronto and begins his medical studies

1898 graduates from medical school at the University of Toronto

1900 leaves Canada to take part in the South African (Second Boer) War (1899–1902)

"To you from failing hands we throw The torch; be yours to hold it high!"

John McCrae: Soldier·Doctor·Poet

1901 travels to Montreal, Quebec, to begin his work at McGill University

1910 accompanies Earl Grey, Canada's governor general, on an expedition to Hudson Bay

1914 joins the British forces at the beginning of the First World War (1914–1918)

MAY 3, 1915 writes the poem "In Flanders Fields"

JANUARY 24, 1918 named as Consulting Physician to the First British Army

JANUARY 28, 1918 dies in Wimereux, France; is buried there the next day

If you see a poppy
And if it nods its head,
Walk softly,
Go around it,
For it marks a soldier's bed.

— Anonymous

GLOSSARY

Armistice: an agreement between enemies to stop fighting; a truce.

Artillery: firing weapons such as cannons and missile launchers. Too heavy to move easily, the weapons are mounted on wheeled bases that can be pulled into position. The troops that use such weapons are also called artillery.

Autopsy: an examination of a dead body to determine the cause of death; a post-mortem.

Battery: a basic unit of soldiers in the artillery.

Boer: a Dutch person or person of Dutch descent living in South Africa; from the Dutch word *boer,* farmer.

Boer War: see South African War.

British Empire: the nations, colonies and protectorates ruled by Great Britain at one time; many of them, such as Canada, India, Australia and New Zealand, are now independent countries.

Concièrge: a person who attends the entrance of a building; a caretaker.

Dressing station: a place for giving emergency treatment to the wounded.

Earl Grey: Sir Albert Grey, 4th Earl Grey (1851–1917), a British nobleman who was governor general of Canada from 1904–1911. While he was in office, Alberta and Saskatchewan entered Confederation in 1905. He invited Newfoundland to join as well.

First World War: (1914–1918) war in which Great Britain (including Canada) and other nations (Allies) defeated Germany and its allied nations; also called the Great War and World War I.

The Front: an army's line or its position closest to the enemy.

Jesuit: a member of a Roman Catholic order, the Society of Jesus.

Kit: set of equipment needed by a soldier.

Lying-in hospital: a hospital where women went to give birth to their babies; before such hospitals were available, babies were born at home.

Magic Lantern: a device once used to project enlarged images of pictures printed on glass slides.

Mess: a room or building where a group of people in the military eat their meals together.

Muskeg: a swamp or bog formed with sphagnum moss and decaying matter, like leaves.

Pathology: the scientific study of the nature of disease, its causes, development and outcome.

Portage: the carrying of boats and supplies overland between two waterways.

Rugby: a field game with similarities to North American football.

South African War: (1899–1902) a war in which Great Britain defeated the Boers of the Orange Free State and the Transvaal Republic in South Africa; the Second Boer War.

Stereogram: a card with two photographs of the same scene, which appear to be three-dimensional.

Victory Bonds: savings bonds sold by the Canadian and British governments to raise money to finance war efforts.

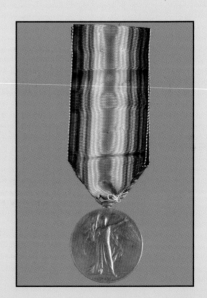

John McCrae, like other veterans in the British Empire, received the Victory Medal. The ribbon's joined rainbows represent the peace brought by the end of the First World War and also the colours of the Allied nations.

ACKNOWLEDGMENTS

The journey to this book began in 1994 and could not have happened without the enthusiastic support of Bev Dietrich, Curator of Guelph Museums in Guelph, Ontario. I thank her for serving as the expert consultant with friendly good cheer and professional candor. Thanks as well to Kathleen Wall, Assistant Curator, who has been ever-ready to send a requested image lickety-split, and to Katherine McCracken, Director of Guelph Museums, who has facilitated so many aspects of this biography.

Heartfelt thanks as well are extended to the terrific crew at Scholastic Canada Ltd.: Sandy Bogart Johnston, a most patient editor and fellow history aficionado; Diane Kerner, supportive publisher; Yüksel Hassan, the designer who made everything look wonderful; and Denise Anderson, doyenne of Marketing and Publicity. Gratitude also goes to David Bennett of The Transatlantic Literary Agency Inc., Toronto; Susan Ross, Canadian War Museum; Mary E. Houde, McGill University Archives; Pamela Miller, Christopher Lyons and Lily Szczygiel, Osler Library of the History of Medicine, McGill University; Phil Dietrich; Lydia Durocher and Cerise Mahuzier, Musée McCord Museum; David Gardner-Medwin; Kathryn Cole; Margaret Beattie, The Sir Andrew Macphail Homestead, Orwell, PEI; Linda Amichand, Archival and Special Collections, University of Guelph; Beau Cooper, Australian War Memorial; Leslie McGrath and Lori Mcleod, The Osborne Collection of Early Children's Books; Fiona O'Connor, Toronto Public Library; Bronwen Quarry, Debra Moore and Andrea McCutcheon, Hudson's Bay Company Archives, Manitoba; Lee Sandstead, art historian; J.R. McKenzie, Curator, RMC Museum, Royal Military College of Canada, Kingston, Ontario; Steve Douglas, The Maple Leaf Legacy Project; Joy and Tristan Heft, Lisgar Collegiate Institute, Ottawa; David Klaassen, Social Welfare History Archives, University of Minnesota; Timothy Dubé, Debbie Jiang and Janet Murray, Library and Archives Canada; Joan O'Malley, Department of Pathology, McGill University; Dr. Richard Fraser, Director, McGill Medical Museum; The City of Toronto Archives.

And finally, as ever, many thanks and much love to Cal, Devon and Brian Smiley, who marched alongside me, through the dark valleys and over the high hills that marked this journey.

John McCrae was born in this stone cottage in Guelph, Ontario, and lived there until he was two years old. The house is a National Historic Site of Canada.

CREDITS

Grateful acknowledgement is made to all those who have granted permission to reprint copyrighted and personal material. Every reasonable effort has been made to locate the copyright holders for these images. The author and publisher would be pleased to receive information that would allow them to rectify any omissions in future printings.

Illustrative materials are from Guelph Museums, except where noted. Items from The Granfield Collection are noted as TGC.

Front cover: (medal and McCrae portrait) Guelph Museums; (other photos) The Granfield Collection (TGC)

Page 1: (poppies) TGC; (right) "In Flanders Fields," John McCrae, Library and Archives Canada C-026561

Page 2: (upper left) TGC; (centre) TGC

Page 3: (upper right) TGC

Page 4: (right) courtesy of The Osborne Collection of Early Children's Books, Toronto Public Library

Page 5: (centre left) TGC

Page 8: (upper left) TGC

Page 10: (lower) SSPL / Science Museum

Page 11: (upper right) CUS_046_009_P, William Osler Photo Collection, Osler Library of the History of Medicine, McGill University, Montreal, Quebec, Canada; (lower) TGC

Page 12: (lower) TGC

Page 13: (upper right) TGC; (lower) *Canadians at Battle of Paardberg, Feb. 1900*, Library and Archives Canada e008319465

Page 14: (upper right) TGC; (inset) TGC

Page 16: (upper left, detail) courtesy of Phil Dietrich

Page 17: (upper right, detail) and page 35 (second from top, detail): Earl Grey's Party at Norway House, 1910, Hudson's Bay Company Archives, Archives of Manitoba, HBCA 1987/363-G-130/128; (lower left) TGC

Page 18: (centre) TGC

Page 20: (upper left and back cover, pin) TGC

Page 21: (upper right) TGC; (upper centre) TGC; (lower right) courtesy of Kathryn Cole

Page 22: (all images) TGC

Page 23: (lower left) Charles Bryant, *Boulogne in Wartime, January 1918*, painting, Oil on Canvas, 73.7 cm x 104.5 cm Australian War Memorial (ART03612); (lower right) surgical instrument set, CWM 19740049-001 © Canadian War Museum

Page 26: (upper left, detail) Officers of the First Brigade, Canadian Field Artillery, Library and Archives Canada C-20188

Page 27: (upper right) courtesy of Lisgar Collegiate Institute, Ottawa, ON; (lower right) TGC

Page 28 and back cover (left): Museé McCord Museum II-229912.0

Page 29: (centre) courtesy of The Maple Leaf Legacy Project

Page 30: (left) Art Historian Lee Sandstead; (upper right, detail) © Bank of Canada, used with permission; (centre) courtesy of Cal Smiley

Page 31: (left, detail) courtesy of McGill Medical Museum, Montreal; (centre and far right) TGC; (lower right) TGC

Page 32: TGC

Page 33: TGC

Page 34: (poppy) TGC; (lower right) courtesy of Social Welfare History Archives, University of Minnesota Libraries, swhp01191

Page 35: (poppy) TGC

Page 38: courtesy of The Maple Leaf Legacy Project

INDEX

BIBLIOGRAPHY

Sir Andrew Macphail. *In Flanders Fields and Other Poems By Lieut.-Col. John McCrae, M.D.* Toronto: William Briggs, 1919.

John F. Prescott. *In Flanders Fields: The Story of John McCrae.* Erin, Ontario: The Boston Mills Press, 1985.

Dianne Graves. *A Crown of Life: The World of John McCrae.* St. Catharines, Ontario: Vanwell Publishing Limited, 1997.

The gravestones in the Wimereux Communal Cemetery, including John McCrae's, lie flat because the soil is too sandy to keep them erect.